Retail Management

Complete Planning & Strategy Framework

Argha Ray

EDITION II

Copyright ©2020 Argha Ray

All rights reserved.

ISBN: 9798669376444

For You………

Contents-

Acknowledgments

Chapter	Title	Page No.
1	Introduction to Retailing Business	1
2	Basics of Retailing	3
3	Consumer Behavior	13
4	Strategy Frameworks	23
5	Retail location	29
6	Store Design	39
7	Merchandise Planning	53
8	Retail Pricing	63
9	Sale Promotion	71
10	HR Management	83
11	Customer Experience	89
12	Retail Analysis	97
13	Online Retailing	103
14	Case Study	109

Acknowledgements

Any accomplishment requires the effort of many people and this work is not different. I thank my parents whose patience and support was instrumental in accomplishing this task.

To all the individuals I have had the opportunity to lead, be led by, or watch their leadership from afar, I want to say thank you for being the inspiration and foundation for this book.

Chapter 1: Introduction to Retailing Business

What is Business? In simple words, the act of providing goods or services in return of capital is known as business. Starting from a local grocery shop to retailers to manufacturing units, several forms of business we come across in our day to day life. Consider our education system. We pay our schools or universities with fees and in return they provide teachers who teach us. Teaching is the service they are providing in return of money, hence this is a business. Automobile companies, they manufacture and sell automobiles in return of money, hence this is a business. Local grocery stores, they sell different products of food items which we need on a daily basis in return of money, hence it is also a business.

When we start talking about business, the very first concept which hits our mind is that business is nothing but purchasing an item at lower rates and selling them at higher rates i.e. retailing. So in this series we are going to discuss about retailing, how to start, complete planning and strategy frameworks, and management.

Chapter 2: Basics of Retailing

The very basic or fundamental goal of any business is to **add values** to your customer's life. It begins by finding a problem which people are facing and solving it so that they become your customers. In retailing also, you try to provide your customers with particular items which they require in their life. Now value is determined as-

Benefits – Cost = Value

Importance of Retailing-

Before we discuss about the importance of retailer or a retailing activity, have a look at the figure given below-

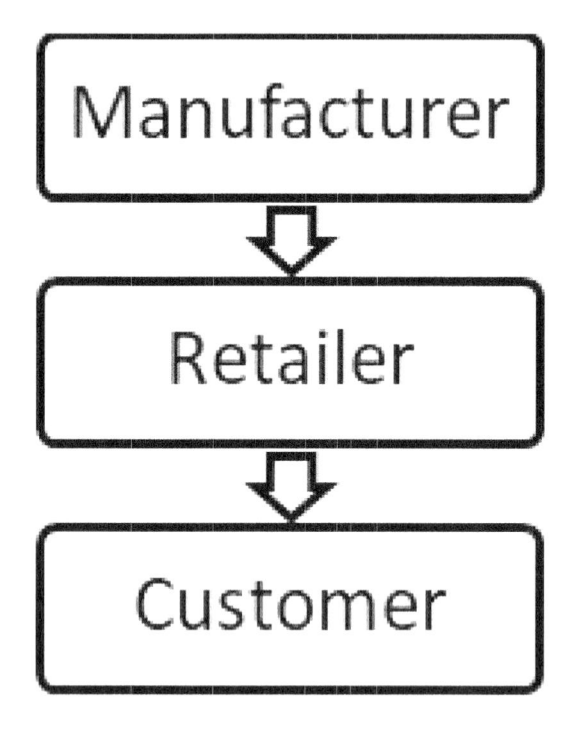

Manufacturer ⇩ Retailer ⇩ Customer

The given figure shows the process of how merchandise or a product moves. Any product is first manufactured in a factory. It is then supplied to its customers. But there are some problems which manufactures and their customers face during this process. For instance, let there be a manufacturing unit situated at Kolkata which produces milk products. But its products are to be supplied to customers all over the country, which is a very difficult job for a single organization to supply products to customers who are too far from Kolkata. Also, for customers who live miles away from Kolkata, it becomes impossible to travel such a large distance only to buy a few products. So distribution of products becomes very difficult.

Now suppose there are some individual organizations from different regions of our country, which collect products in bulk from the manufacturer as per demand in their region and then distribute it to the customers in their region. In this case, product supply process becomes much easier and affordable. This role of distribution is played by retailers. The manufacturer supplies these retailers through their distributers.

Every retail operations follow a common business model. It is known as **AIDAA** model. AIDAA stands for-

Awareness -> **I**nterest -> **D**esire -> **A**ction -> **A**dvocacy

AIDAA model describes the basic processes of retailing-

1. Awareness- you need to first establish your retail organization in the market and make people aware about your existence.
2. Interest- after creating awareness, you need to create interest in people's mind about your organization so that they choose you over your competitors.
3. Desire- now you need to create desire in them to make a purchase from your organization.
4. Action- now the actual buying process happens. Your customers come to you to buy a product.

5. Advocacy- after the product has been purchased; you need to now analyse your customer's post purchase behavior, whether they are satisfied or not, if there's anything else that the customer was expecting from you, etc.

These are basic guidelines which you shall follow to setup a successful retailing organization. Now there are several methods which we can use for these guidelines. For example, to make people aware of your existence you can advertise about your company. Many a time customers' post purchase behaviors are observed and actions are taken to make them completely satisfied. This is because if your existing customers are satisfied, they will recommend other people to visit your organization. This is known as **word of mouth.** It brings you more customers without investing anything extra on advertising. That is why **Advocacy** is so important.

There are three **channels** through which retail operations can be performed-

1. Offline channel
2. Online channel
3. Omni channel

Offline channel is a channel where the customer needs to be physically present at a physical location to make a purchase. For example- a restaurant where a customer needs to be physically present to have the food.

Online channel is a channel where the customers don't need to visit any physical location. They can purchase their product through an online store. For example- an e-commerce platform like Amazon or Flipkart.

Both offline and online channels have their own pros and cons. To make use of benefits of both the channels some companies use **Omni channel**. In this channel a company has both a physical store as well as an e-commerce platform. For example- 'Lenskart' is a company that has both an online selling channel and physical stores.

But, which channel will be beneficial for your retailing organization depends upon the kind of merchandise you are selling. For instance- in case of large electronics like air conditioners or air coolers the customer prefers to visit a physical showroom to have a look at the product, decide which model suits his room the most and then only make the deal. Similarly in case of garments the customer prefers to visit the store to touch and feel the quality of the dress material. On the other hand, products like an e-book; in this case an online store will be preferred more over a physical showroom. We will discuss about these channels in details later on.

There are 4 basic components of retailing-

1. **Product-** you need to decide very wisely what kind of product you want to sell, product whose demand is considerably high over other products in your retailing location. For example- if you set up a non-veg restaurant in a region where people prefers veg food only, then you can never expect any profit.

2. **Price-** you need to decide at which price point you will sell your merchandise. If your target market or target customers are middle class families but you try to sell them very expensive products, you are most likely to have no customers at all.
3. **Place-** you need to select a physical location to setup your store in such a way that customers get an easy access of your location.
4. **Promotion-** this is a vital component which many retailers ignore. We will have a separate chapter on this topic only.

Difference between variety and assortment-

- **Variety-** different categories of products.
- **Assortment-** number of different categories under the same category.

For example- let there be a large electronic retailing organization. It sells televisions, air conditioners and washing machine. So it has 3 varieties of merchandise. For television, it sells televisions of 4 different manufacturers. So it has an assortment of 4 under the category of television.

Retail Image-

Retail image can be simply understood as the impression about your retail organization in people's mind. What kind of product you sell, what are your price ranges, location of your store, general display of your store, your target market, your target customers, what kind of post purchase services you provide etc. decides your retail image. A good retail image helps the business to grow but a poor retail image causes the business to die out.

Services-

After you have successfully created a good retail image, it is now time to provide your customers with good services. There are basically 3 categories of services that are provided-

1. **Self service-** where the entire process is carried out by the customer himself. For example a large FMCG store where variety of products are arranged on different shelves. A customer walks in, picks up the products by himself and then goes to the

billing counter for payment. No additional services are provided to him.
2. **Limited service-** where the customer is provided with some sorts of services, like a sales person who guides the customer through different products.
3. **Full service-** here the customer is provided with all sorts of services, including post purchase services.

After deciding the kind of services you want to provide, it is important to do some **retail analysis** to figure your weak points and areas of improvements which will help you to optimize your net profit and grow your business.

We will discuss each of those above mentioned topics in details in our subsequent chapters. In the next chapter we are going to discuss about consumer behaviors, which will help us to form different retailing strategies to maximize our profit.

Chapter 3: Consumer Behavior

To dominate the market it is important to understand the market. And the best way to understand the market is to understand consumer behaviors. Consumers have some expectations from the market. If your retail organization can fulfill their expectations then only they will choose you over your competitors.

Suppose you have purchased a new 2bhk flat. But in summers it becomes too hot. It becomes very difficult to stay in your flat during the day. You need to find a solution for this. What will you do? Definitely you will follow the following steps-

1. First, you will try to search for a solution for this problem. An air conditioner would be an ideal choice in this case. So you have decided to buy a new air conditioner for your room.
2. Next, you will try to figure out which air conditioner model would be perfect for you. You are basically searching for

information about various air conditioners available.
3. Next, you would like to find a dealer from whom you can buy the air conditioner. You came across several retailers near you who sell air conditioners. You decide which one of them is the best based on the price range they offer, their product quality and services provided.
4. Now you visit the retailer and purchase your air conditioner.
5. Now comes the vital part, your satisfaction. After you start using the machine, you try to figure out if you are satisfied or not, whether the services provided by the retailer were as per your expectations or not. Based on that, if you are satisfied, then you will stick to the same retailer for further purchases. In case if you are not satisfied, then you are most likely to switch to any other retailer.

We can now see that product purchase is actually a five step process-

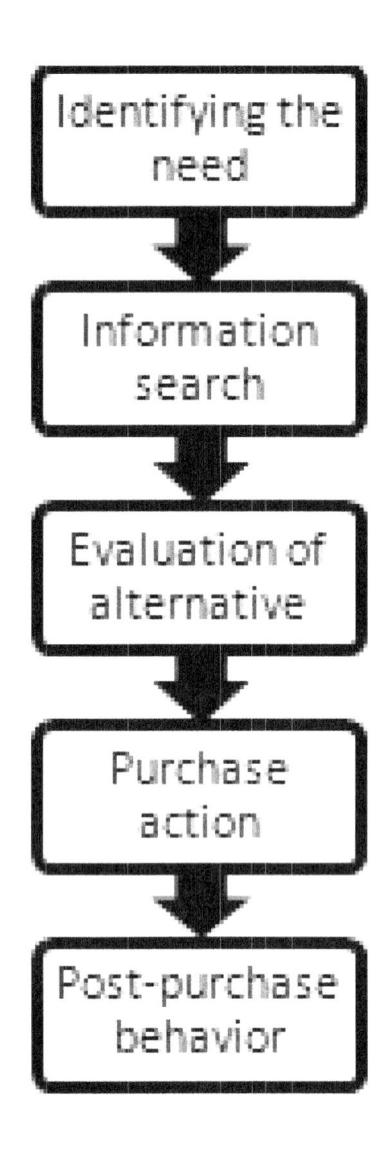

```
Identifying the need
        ↓
Information search
        ↓
Evaluation of alternative
        ↓
Purchase action
        ↓
Post-purchase behavior
```

- First the customer identifies the product which he needs.
- Then he tries to gather more information about the product.
- Then he looks for retailers and selects the best among them.
- He then purchases the product.
- After purchasing, the customer decides whether he is satisfied or not and based on that decides whether to stick to the same retailer for future purchases or switch to some other retailer.

Now to dominate the market, you need to contribute to each of these steps. You have to make a customer's product purchase behavior more satisfying and comfortable. Then only customers are more likely to choose you or your retail organization every time they plan to buy something.

In the first step, you need to understand what people out there are looking for. For example, if it is winter season, people are most likely to buy room heaters and geysers instead of air conditioners. So if you are an electronics retailer, you need to bring new stocks of room heaters and geysers. You need to understand their needs.

In the second step, a customer is looking for information about the product. Many retailers take advantage of this situation. Many a time people use the internet for gathering information. If you can somehow use the internet to provide information about the products your customers are looking for, then there is a high probability that customers would select your retail store for the product in order to reduce their effort. For example- if they you provide their required information, say it be mechanical and price details about a room heater, along with your retail locations phone number and the price you are offering, then in order to save time and effort they are most likely to call your retail store for the product.

In the third step, evaluation of alternatives, your customers are now comparing the prices of the product that different retailers are offering. There you need to hit the market by providing the best price.

In the fourth step, purchase action, the customer purchases the product form you. Here you are required to provide him with all sorts of services in order to satisfy all his expectations. Then only you can expect a good image about your organization.

In the last step, after using the product, the customer might be having some sort of complaint about the product. He might want you to solve that problem. Here if you can respond as quickly as possible to his feedback, the customer feels more satisfied and you end up building a good relationship with that customer. Next time he needs to buy any other product he is going to choose you over your competitors. Remember, a customer complaints and gives feedback only because he wants to stick to you. And you need to respect that.

There is something called **customer retention rate**. Before understanding this, note down some points-

- It is easier to do business with existing customer.

- A lot of capital is required to acquire new customers.
- Old or existing customers tend to spend a lot more than new customers because of good relationships between them and the retailer.
- Old or existing customers often help to gather new customers through **word of mouth** (discussed earlier).

So you can see that old or existing customers are actually great assets to retailers. And thus it is very important to retain these customers, make sure that they stick to your company and indirectly help your company to grow. **Customer retention rate** is defined as the percentage of customers who are still doing business with your retail organization at the end of one year about the total number of customers at the beginning of the year. For example- suppose in a particular year, you had 200 customers at the beginning. At the end of that particular year, you are left with 150 customers. So your customer retention rate is

(150/200) X 100% = **75%**

If this rate is higher than 100%, it is a good sign of growth in business. If it is less than 100%, then you need to focus on the customers post-purchase behaviors. In order to save money on acquiring new customers, you need to focus on existing customers; therefore your customer's satisfaction level is a very crucial factor which you should focus on.

In order to retain customers, retailers use many strategies like- asking for feedback after the purchase and take necessary actions as soon as possible, making them aware of new products, deals and offers through emails or text messages, giving them special discounts, offering new membership schemes, etc.

Speaking of behavior, we discussed about general steps which a consumer follows in order to buy a product. But during the actual purchase process, a consumer needs to deal with two kinds of situations-

1. **Contemplated purchase-** in this situation the customer is preplanned about the product he wants to buy. He has a particular model in his mind. He walks in

the store, asks the store personal for the product, and buys it.
2. **Impulse purchase-** in this situation the customer might or might not be preplanned about the product. He walks in the store, asks the store personal about the product he needs. Now the store personal tries to introduce to the customer some more products which are more expensive and tries to make him buy those products.

Impulse purchase strategies are quite risky. This is because if the sales person is trying to be very pushy then the customer may feel very uncomfortable, make no purchase and you end up losing a customer and build up a bad reputation of your company.

In this chapter we learned about customer purchase behaviors and understood why they are an important asset to a retail organization. In our next chapter, we are going to discuss about how to frame strategies.

Chapter 4: Strategy Frameworks

As discussed earlier, a retail operation consists of several factors, and solid plans and strategies are required to excel in those areas. But above all, every operation has a target, a goal, an objective. Before establishing a retail organization, we must have clear vision of what we are looking for, what are our targets. Then we need to plan necessary actions to be taken to achieve our goals. A retail organization is a team. Thus each and every member of that team must work together for their common goal.

Many startups fail at its initial days only due to various reasons like- poor management, poor quality and choice of products, no after purchase support, no loyalty plans, bad behavior of employees, etc. Whether a retail organization is going to sustain in the market or not depends upon 5 crucial factors-

1. Values added to customer's life.

2. Services which are rare.
3. Operating strategies and plans which are unique and inimitable.
4. Whether operations are well organized or not.
5. Ability to update the system or way of operating.

A customer would like to do business with you only if you can add values to his life. Otherwise there's no point of wasting his time on your organization. To make sure he keeps visiting your store only over your competitors you must provide him with unique and rare services which are not provided by your competitors. In order to maximize your profit you must be having some operating strategies which your competitors can not use due to other financial factors. You also need to make sure that that retail organization is well organized and the customer doesn't face any problem in the purchase process. Also, you need to keep updating your ways of operating based on current and future scenarios to always stay updated and flow with the trend.

There are several elements of retailing where wise decisions are required to be made and strategies are framed accordingly. These elements are known as **retail mix elements-**

1. Location of retail store
2. Format
3. Layout and visual merchandise
4. Merchandise type
5. Merchandising policy
6. Pricing policy
7. Private label v/s national brands
8. Promotional strategies
9. Information technology
10. Supply chain management
11. Human resource management
12. Services and experience
13. Customer relationships

There are three fundamental strategies and you need to select any one of them in order to make further plans-

1. **Blue ocean strategy-** where you try to create an uncontested market place. It is like you are the only bait in the entire ocean and all fishes i.e. customers come only to

you to have the bait. You are something unique and no other can imitate you.
2. **Scenario based strategy-** where you analyse your competitors and try to imitate then in order to compete against them.
3. **AAT strategy-** AAT or Act According to Trend is a strategy where you try to sell hottest and trendy products, offer cheapest price, easiest and quickest ways to access the product.

Sometimes, after executing a strategy you may find that it is not working as expected. In such situations you need to change or modify the strategy to meet your expectations. In case your targets are not achieved you need to find out areas of improvement and plan your investments accordingly. The best way for this is to seek help of **retail analysis**. You need to analyse several areas, find out how much to invest in each area and make plans accordingly. Some of them are-

1. Total revenue generated
2. Margins from each category of products
3. Gross margin per sale

4. Gross margin with respect to capital spent on inventory
5. Gross margin return per employee
6. Gross margin return on square footage
7. Return on investments
8. Return on assets
9. Category of customers
10. Revenue generated from each category of customers

We need to analyse different aspects of our business on a regular basis in order to optimize our profit. We will have an entire chapter on retail analysis. But before that, after deciding what kind of merchandise we are going to sell, we need to now look for a good location where we can establish our retail store. In the next chapter we are going to discuss about site decision.

Chapter 5: Retail Location

Definition- Retail location or a trading area is a geographic area containing customers of a particular retail group or a group of retail organizations for a specific group of goods and services.

Basically it is physical store where a customer walks in and buys the product. In case of online retailing we don't need such a store. But if you remember, we have discussed earlier that in some cases consumers prefer offline stores over online platforms. Hence, we need to have broad discussion on this topic.

Since your retail store is the first point of actual interaction between you and your customers, it creates the first impression about your retail organization in your customers' mind, which ultimately adds to your retail image. In order to create a good impression and generate good amount of sales you need to make sure that your store site is easily accessible, located at a busy area where your store gets a lot of exposure, near an area where most of the people are your target customers. Buying or renting a physical piece of land is very expensive and unlike financial decisions site location decision is not flexible. Once you have established your store on a location, it becomes very difficult to change it because lot money is involved in the process. So, you need to select a plot of land very wisely in this case.

You need to consider some factors before deciding your retail store location-

1. **Population size and traits-** as discussed in one of the earlier chapters, if you sell non-veg food in a location where people prefer veg food only, then you cannot expect any income from that area. Ideally, a retail store must be set up in an area where population density is very high and they demand products that your organization sells.
2. **Competition-** when you select any plot, you need to look whether any competitors are present or not in that area. Sometimes it becomes beneficial if there are competitors

if you are able to provide better quality of products and services. But on the other hand, if you can't, then you can very well understand the consequences.

3. **Nature of nearby stores-** sometimes nearby stores which are not your competitors might help you to get customers indirectly. For example- suppose your store sells ladies jewelries. And your nearby stores sell ladies garments. After a customer purchases a dress of any of those stores, she is most likely to visit your store for jewelries which she can wear along with that dress. So their customers become your customers.

4. **Property cost-** in order to save investment money, you need to consider the cost of the plot as well.

5. **Legal restrictions-** before buying a plot make sure there are no legal restrictions against setting up a retail store.

6. **Essential services-** you need to ensure that your area is provided with essential services like 24X7 power supply, proper water supply, etc.

7. **Transportation access-** you need to ensure that transportation in your area is smooth and effortless as there's going to be a lot of transportation activities like product delivery to customers, product receiving from manufacturers and distributors, etc.

Trading Area Analysis-

Just like retail analysis, before we select any retail location, we need to analyse the plot in order to make maximum profit. There are two models that we are going to use for analyzing-

1. Analog model
2. Gravitational model

There is another model, known as **regression model.** But this model is quite complex and difficult to implement. So we will stick to analog and gravitational models only.

Analog model

In this model, potential sales for a new store are estimated based on sales of similar stores in existing area.

It mainly talks about similar retailers who are already having their stores in that area. Sometimes having a lot of similar stores in an area attracts the customer to visit that area as he gets a lot of choices. It makes the area more popular and more and more people start visiting that area. If your selected area has similar stores as discussed in the case of garments and jewelries, then such stores acts as supplement to your store and increases your sales. Also if there are your competitors and you know that their customers are extremely unsatisfied by their services, then you might select that area if you can offer your customers better product at better price range with better services. At the same time, if you cannot offer better services then you should look for another area because customers hesitate to switch their choices.

Analog model is a primitive model which is not much scientific. This is based on simple observation and customer psychology and a bit of luck only. Nowadays retailers use more scientific models.

Gravitational model-

Unlike analog model, gravitational models are modern and more scientific. There are two gravitational models that we are going to discuss-

1. Reilly's law of retail gravitation
2. Huff's law of retail gravitation

1. Reilly's gravitation model-

Suppose there are two similar shops in a locality situated at some particular distance apart. Both of them sell same variety of products. This law helps to determine the point between their physical length of separation where a customer decides to choose which store needs to be visited.

Suppose there are two similar retail stores A and B. Both of them sale similar products. Only their physical dimensions are different. They are 10km apart from each other as shown below-

A ←——————→ 10km ←——————→ B

Let,

- d_{AB} = distance from A to B where the customer decides to choose which store needs to be visited.
- d = distance between A and B. In this case d is 10km.
- a = maximum number of customers that can shop in store A at any particular period of time. In this case let a=10,000.
- b = maximum number of customers that can shop in store B at any particular period of time. In this case let a=2,000.

Then by Reilly's gravitational model,

$$d_{AB} = d/(1 + \sqrt{\frac{a}{b}})$$

In this case, putting the values of d, a and b in the above equation we get d_{AB} = 6.89km. So if you are retailer A and retailer B is your competitor, then you need to make sure d_{AB} has a high value so that your effective area of acquiring customers is greater than that of B.

2. Huff's gravitational model-

Suppose there are three retail stores selling identical products. But their areas of store are different. There is a customer who can access all of these stores, one at a time. Distances of each of these stores from his home are different as well. Huff's gravitational model gives us the probability of the customer coming from his home to these stores.

Let us understand this by an example. Suppose there are three stores, A, B and C. Area of store A, B and C are 1000 square feet, 250 square feet and 1800 square feet respectively. For a customer, it takes 10 minutes, 5 minutes and 15 minutes to visit store A, B and C respectively from his home. So by Huff's law, probability of customer coming from home to a particular store is given by-

$$P_i = \{s_i/t_i\} \div \{\Sigma\{s_i/t_i\}\}$$

- P_i = required probability
- t_i = time required to come to the store from home
- s_i = area of the store

In this case, putting all the values to the above equation, probability of customer coming to store A, B and C are 0.37, 0.185 and 0.445 respectively. Clearly store C, in spite of having a greater distance, gets the advantage here.

In this chapter we learned about deciding site location, different models of site location, analysis of location, etc. Now that we have selected a retail location, it is time to build the store and design it. In the next chapter we are going to discuss about store design and layout in order to make your retail store look more attractive and convenient. Before that, please revise the models described in this chapter once again.

Chapter 6 Store Design

Once you have successfully built your store, now it's time to arrange it. See, when a customer walks in your store, your store visuals creates the first impression about you in your customer's mind. If it is a positive impression then selling products to the customer becomes much easier.

The motive of this chapter is to learn how to create necessary **atmospherics**. It is the psychological feeling a customer gets when visiting a retailer. It starts from the very exterior of the store and ends once the customer steps out.

There are four different elements of store design-

1. Exterior
2. General interior
3. Interior displays
4. Store layout

Exterior-

You might have noticed that the exterior of a store is beautifully designed. It looks clean, appealing, beautiful entrances, and some facilities like car parking. Even if people are not familiar with your retail store, they may decide to visit your store as the exterior looks so appealing. In such cases impulse purchase strategy becomes very effective.

There are basically three components of exterior designing-

i. Storefront
ii. Entrances
iii. Facilities provided

Storefront describes the look of the store exterior. Many retailers in order to make the store more attractive and special use different signage, interesting colour on the walls of store, symbols, etc. For example, you might have noticed what McDonald's outlets use. On every outlet of McDonald's exterior you can see their giant 'M' logo in yellow, and sometimes a clown sitting on a bench. This makes the store look very unique and creates an impression in its customer's mind that the food here is very tasty.

Entrances also play a great role here. The type of entrance, number of entrances and size of entrances actually adds up to your **retail image**. Not only retail image but it is also important for controlling the flow of customers in and out of the store. For example, some retailing stores have only one entrance door but it is very wide. This often indicates that the store is selling expensive products. Apple stores have wide but single entrances. On the other hand, a narrow entrance indicated that the store is selling affordable items. Sometimes wide entrances are also used to display the products inside as much as possible to outside people to attract them. Sometimes wide entrances are also required in case there is a huge volume of customers entering and leaving the store at a time.

Sometimes more than one entrance are required. For example, in large FMCG stores, you may notice that there is an entry gate where customers enter and there's an exit gate where billing counter is situated. In order to maintain security, customers are expected to leave the store only through the exit after paying for their products.

In order to make store access much easier and convenient, some facilities like car parking are also provided outside the store. Such services add to customer satisfaction.

General Interior-

Once a customer enters the store, he now expects good atmospherics, good lighting so that the products are easily visible, etc. In order to create good atmospherics and display the products better, following general interior components should be kept in mind-

i. Floorings
ii. Lightings
iii. Store fixtures
iv. Aisle spaces
v. Personnel
vi. Merchandise arrangement
vii. Cleanliness

Flooring and lightings should be selected very wisely because bright lights with light coloured floorings make the store looks much brighter and products are more easily visible.

You also need to make sure that aisle space, where the customer actually interacts with store personnel or the displayed product is very convenient and appealing.

Looks of store personnel also affects your impression in your customers' mind. For example, a man in suit or proper formal attire looks more professional and trustworthy than a man in casual wears.

How you display your merchandise also affects your customer's decision on whether to buy the product or not. For example, if you as a customer see that the products are displayed in a very haphazard manner they you may not feel them very appealing and decide to leave the store.

Several customers visit your store throughout the day. So it is also important to maintain overall store cleanliness and hygiene throughout the day.

Interior Displays-

While general interior talks about the overall looks of the store interior, **interior display** gives us ideas on how to make a customer approach a product and buy it.

There are several tricks that retailers use regarding interior displays. They use attractive **signage, featured areas, end caps, live demo or presentation of merchandise**, etc.

Next time you visit the market, try to find out what kind of **signage** do retailers generally use. There are two types of signage-

i. **Category-** such type of signage shows the category of products the retailer is selling. They are often used to guide the customers to part of the store they should go in order to purchase a particular kind of product.

ii. **Promotional-** such type of signage displays different offers and discounts offered on a product and new arrivals. You might have noticed some sign boards in a store showing '60% OFF' or something like 'BUY 2 GET 1

FREE'. These are meant to promote the product and increase sales.

Sometimes you may notice that there are some areas within the store which has been decorated based on a particular product or particular brand only. Such areas are known as **featured areas.** Such plans are used to attract customers to products which are brand new and not very popular. Sometimes manufacturers pay the retailers to display their new products separately in their stores in order to make the products popular and increase its demand.

In some FMCG stores, you may notice that at the end of a row of products organized on shelves, when the customer is about to turn and enters a new row, there is a separate small section which is dedicated to a particular product only, which is known as **end cap**. This is a brilliant idea which uses human psychology. By the time a customer comes at the end of a row, he loses all his interest on previous products and expects something new. At that moment, getting a new product all of a sudden makes him very interested on that very particular product. Thus there is a high chance that the customer might pick up that product and buy it. End caps are generally used for newer products or products which are generally slow moving.

Sometimes live **demonstrations** are also given on how to use a product, what are its capabilities and functions, etc. For example, sometimes a store personnel is hired to demonstrate the use of a particular product, like vacuum cleaner. It shows that the vacuum cleaner is very efficient and worth the price.

Store Layout-

Now that we know how to display our merchandise, it is now time to understand how to arrange them and optimise our store space utilisation. In order to do that, we need to learn about store layout.

In a store, we can divide the floor space in 4 fundamental categories-

  i. Selling space
 ii. Merchandise space
iii. Personnel space
 iv. Customer space

Selling space is where the products are put on display. Products are often displayed on shelves as in FMCG store, or on walls as in case of air conditioners, or glass show cases as in case of jewelries, etc. Usually most of the store space is actually utilised as selling space.

Merchandise space is commonly known as inventory or storeroom for the store. In every retailing store, one portion of the store is accessible to customers, which is used to display products, while the other portion is used as a storage room where other products are kept. For example, suppose in an electronic store, which sells laptops. You may observe that laptops of various brands are displayed in the store. You select one which you wish to buy, and then a man goes into the merchandise space to bring a new laptop of the same model and gives it to you.

Personnel space is the space which is accessible only to store staffs. They use it for taking rest, keep their essentials, washrooms, etc. This area is not accessible to customers.

Customer space is the space which a customer can physically access, like the space where a customer stands in order interact with the product or store personnel, cash counter, customer waiting area, etc.

We can determine how much space do we need as personnel space, how much space do we need for merchandise space, but, the question is, "how much floor space to assign for selling and customer?" If we can wisely calculate selling space, remaining becomes the customer space. For determining selling space we generally use two methods-

1. **Model stock approach-** determines the floor space necessary to carry and display a proper merchandise assortment. This method is based on the physical space that your merchandise actually needs to display itself properly. This allows us to display more products at a time.
2. **Sales productivity ratio-** assigns floor space on the basis of sales or profit per square foot. Different variety or assortment of products gives different profit margins, different amount of sales. Take different products and compare the profit you make

form each of them. The product which gives more profit and more easily sold is given more space than other products.

Now that we know how to assign floor space, it is now time to understand **traffic flow control** within the store. This explains how you want your customers to move within your retail store. This is required to ensure a smooth flow of traffic, customer satisfaction and security of merchandise. There are three traffic flow layouts generally used-

1. **Grid layout-** here products are arranged in long parallel rows in such a manner that once a customer enters a row, he is expected to enter the next row only after finishing with the current row. A very common example of such a layout can be observed in FMCG stores. One advantage of this layout is that the customer is indirectly forced to go through a large variety or assortment of products. This sometimes makes the customer buy some extra items which was out of his list.

Retail Management

Cash Counter	SHELF 1	
	SHELF 2	
	SHELF 3	
	SHELF 4	

Grid Layout

2. **Free form-** here products are arranged and placed randomly in the store. Such a layout is usually observed in small boutiques. This layout makes the store look very attractive, but on the other hand also becomes difficult for the customer to search for a particular category of product.
3. **Race track layout-** here different categories of products are placed at different sections of the entire selling space in such a way that a customer who is in a particular section can move to any other section without actually bothering about other unnecessary sections.

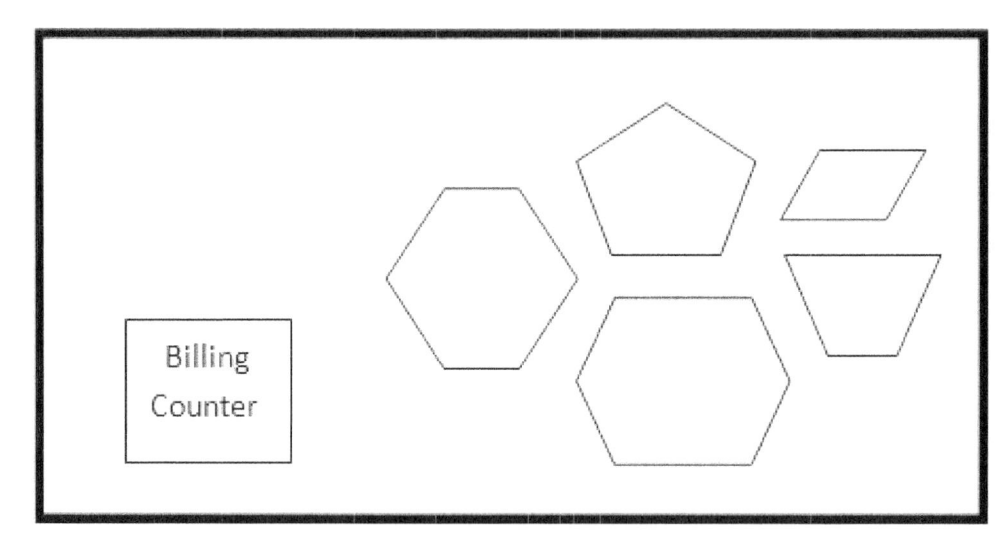

Race Track Layout

Chapter 7: Merchandise Planning

After successfully planning all of store exterior and interior, it is now time to bring actual merchandises in the store. We have already decided what sort of products we are going to sell. Suppose we want to sell electronics, but what category or variety or assortment of electronics. For that we need a solid merchandise plan.

In order to plan your merchandises, there are some guiding principles which we need to follow-

1. Target market
2. Retailer type
3. Value provided
4. Supplier capabilities
5. Cost
6. Competitor
7. Product trend

The kind of product you are planning to sell depends highly on your **target market.** There are very expensive products which only rich customers can afford. Some products are also there which are affordable but their quality is not as good as those expensive products. These products are purchased more by customers belonging to the middle class section of the market. Majority of the market is actually occupied by such customers. So your very first step in merchandise planning is to select your target market, because you cannot sell high end luxury products to middle class customers or sell affordable products to customers who seek luxury. For instance, if you plan to sell cars, then you can never sell luxurious limousines to middle class people. They want something which they can afford, like everyday hatchbacks.

After selecting your target market, you need to see if it is compatible with your **retail image** or not. For example, suppose you have created a perception in your customer's mind that you sell products of a very high quality, but instead you sell very cheap and poor quality products, then you are going to lose customers and get a very low customer retention rate. If such situation occurs, then you need to give a lot of effort along with huge investments either to change the products or bring customers or change your retail image. Sometimes it works, but most of the time, such efforts fail to give you desired results.

Any business becomes successful only if, at the end of the day, is able to provide **value** to its customers. If it is of no use for people, then how can someone expect people to take interest in it? Whatever merchandise you wish to sell, make sure, that it is able to provide some values your customer's life. It must be solving some sort of problem of your customer.

Supplier capability is a factor that should also be kept in mind. Merchandises are supplied to your retail store by some suppliers. In a retail operation, there is a flow of merchandise, starting from the manufacturer, to the supplier, to retailer and finally to the end consumer. Now if somehow this chain gets disrupted, the entire retail operation gets hampered. Suppose you are selling a product which is very fast moving or has a very high demand in the market. You have a supplier who supplies you that particular product. But the quantity of products that the supplier is able to supply can't match the current demand. Hence when a customer walks in your store for the product, and finds out that it is out of stock, it creates a very high level of dissatisfaction for the customer and affects your retail image. You need to select your supplier very wisely. You need to make sure that your supplier is capable of providing you as much products as you require.

No matter how good your product is, if it is not priced well, no one's going to buy it. When a customer thinks about buying a product, after gathering all necessary information about it, he looks for its **cost.** Now one category of product or one particular product is often sold by many retailers. The customer selects that retail only who charges a reasonable price for the product. So you need to charge accordingly. Sometimes if you charge a very low price on a particular product, the customer often starts to think that the quality of the product is very poor as bad quality products are very cheap. In order to understand it better, we will be having a separate chapter on retail pricing strategy.

If there is no challenge in life, there is no life at all. And one of the biggest challenges in retailing is your **competitors.** In order to perform well in the competition, you need to observe your competitors very well, what kind of promotional strategies are they using, what kind of products are they bringing to their store, any new variety or assortment of products or not, what kind of prices they are offering, what kind of discounts are they offering, etc. You need to observe them, learn from them, and bring something new to compete against them. If both of you and your competitors are selling same products, then you need to make sure that your services are better than theirs, your prices are better than theirs, etc.

Remember we talked about trends in stock market? We learned why it is so important to observe and analyse the trend in order to maximize the profit. Similarly, in retailing, observing the **product trend** is important in order to select the product you need to add in or remove from your retail store. In order to make maximum profit you need to sell products which are trendy, have a very high demand and fast moving, i.e. are easily sold. This can be done by understanding the trend, what kind of products do customers prefer, which brand they prefer the most, etc.

Now that we have properly planned our merchandise, it is now time to actually buy the merchandise for selling. There are seven steps you need to follow for merchandise buying-

1. **Gathering information-** before you buy your merchandises, you need to plan for the exact quantity of merchandise you require. If you face a situation of stock out, then it is going to hamper your retail image. At the same time, if your stock is way more than it is actually being sold, you have to face a great loss and it will become difficult to bring new products in the store as the store inventory is not clear out of previous products. So you need to again go to the basics of market analysis as discussed earlier and predict your sales. It is not an easy job. Again, after you have planned the quantity, it is now time to look for suppliers who are able to provide you with that quantity of merchandise at the right time.

Make sure that your supplier has a license for his job.

2. **Interaction with merchandise source-** after selecting your supplier, you need to now contact him for supply. Sometimes, smaller manufacturers do not have suppliers, they supply products on their own. Whatever the case is, you need to now contact him for prices involved.

3. **Evaluation-** the supplier has given you his terms and pricelist. You need to now evaluate if this price is suitable to your budget or not. You need to think whether he is charging you a lot or not. If you are not comfortable with his prices, you need to now look for another supplier who can offer you a better price.

4. **Negotiation-** before making the final deal with your supplier, you should always try to negotiate with him and try to reduce the price as much as possible. Sometimes, if the retailer is very small with respect to the supplier, it becomes difficult to negotiate because the supplier is more powerful here. Similarly, if the retailer is very big in terms

of sales and net profit with respect to the supplier, it becomes very easy to negotiate and reduce the price because the retailer in this case is more powerful.

5. **Purchasing-** the final deal is made and the merchandise is purchased.
6. **Receiving and stocking-** the supplier now delivers the product to your desired place. You can either ship it to your merchandise place or your showroom area.
7. **Reordering of merchandise-** since it takes some time for delivery of merchandise from supplier to retailer, you need to reorder your merchandise at the right time before you get out of stock.

So in this chapter, we learned about merchandise planning, how to select our ideal category of products, learnt some guiding principles, learned the impact of our target market, competitors, product trend, type of retailer or retail image, supplier capabilities on merchandise selection, how to select a supplier, importance of evaluation of price and negotiation, and proper timing of reordering etc.

Once the merchandise arrives at the store, the next step is to decide at what price point we need to sell it in order to maximize our profit. In the next chapter we are going to learn about different pricing strategies commonly used by retailers in order to maximize merchandise flow and profit.

Chapter 8: Retail Pricing

In this we are going to discuss about some pricing strategies and price adjustment techniques. You might have noticed, that some retailers offer a very low price throughout the year, while some other retailers offer different prices at different seasons of the year. Ever wondered why they do so? These are some pricing strategies that we are going to discuss.

There are three fundamental pricing techniques-

1. Demand oriented
2. Competitive oriented
3. Cost oriented

Demand Oriented-

This is a case when a retailer charges as much as customers are willing to pay. Of course you cannot sell above MRP, but you can keep your profit margin as very high. This is generally the case when demand for a particular product is very high. In order to take full advantage of the situation, retailers charge a very high price, because they know, whatever the price is, he is still going to have customers as demand is very high. For example, at the beginning of winter season, the demand for warm clothing is very high, so is the price. By the end of winter season, when there is very less or no demand, retailers, in order to clear their inventory and bring new clothes for summer season, put their winter collection at sale charging very low prices.

Competitive Oriented-

Here, a retailer sets the price depending upon the prices set by his competitors. At the end of the day, in general, a customer is always attracted to that retailer who offers lowest price for a particular product. Competitive oriented pricing is most of the time beneficial, but keep in mind, if the retailer sets a price which is very low, it sometimes creates a perception in customers' minds that the product might be of very poor quality and obsolete. If this happens, even though the price is lower than its competitors, that retailer will not be able to make any sale.

Cost Oriented-

Here, the retailer offers a fixed price throughout the year, or for some other shorter duration. There are basically two cost oriented pricing strategies-

i. Every Day Low Pricing (EDLP)
ii. High-Low Pricing (HiLo)

Every Day Low Pricing (EDLP)-

In this strategy, a retailer sets a fixed price, which is much lower than the market price of a product, throughout the year. For example, many pharmacies in India offer a fixed discount on their medicines throughout the year. Many FMCG stores also use EDLP.

The main purpose of EDLP is to attract as many customers as possible. But there are some factors to be considered before using this strategy-

- Consider your **target market** first. EDLP is generally meant for customers who belong to the middle class category, who love buying products if offered at a lesser price than the market price. If your target market is status oriented, or rich customers, who love to enjoy luxury and spend on costly products, then EDLP is not an ideal choice.

- Next, restrictions on **price elasticity.** Once you have applied EDLP, but the profit is not as much as you had expected, then it becomes very difficult to increase the price. This is because, often customers are price sensitive. Once they find out that you have increased your price, they will start looking for an alternative where they can still buy the same product at lesser price, and your competitors may take advantage of this situation.

High-Low Pricing (HiLo)-

In this strategy, a retailer increases or decreases the price with time. Sometimes the price is very high, and rest of the time it is very low. Then what is the difference between HiLo and demand oriented pricing? In demand oriented pricing, in a particular season, or in a time span, the prices comes down gradually, but in HiLo pricing, the price remains constant throughout the season or time span and falls down suddenly at the end of the season.

If we compare EDLP and HiLo pricing strategies, then, for the same product, the high price in HiLo is higher than EDLP price and the low price of HiLo is lesser than that of EDLP.

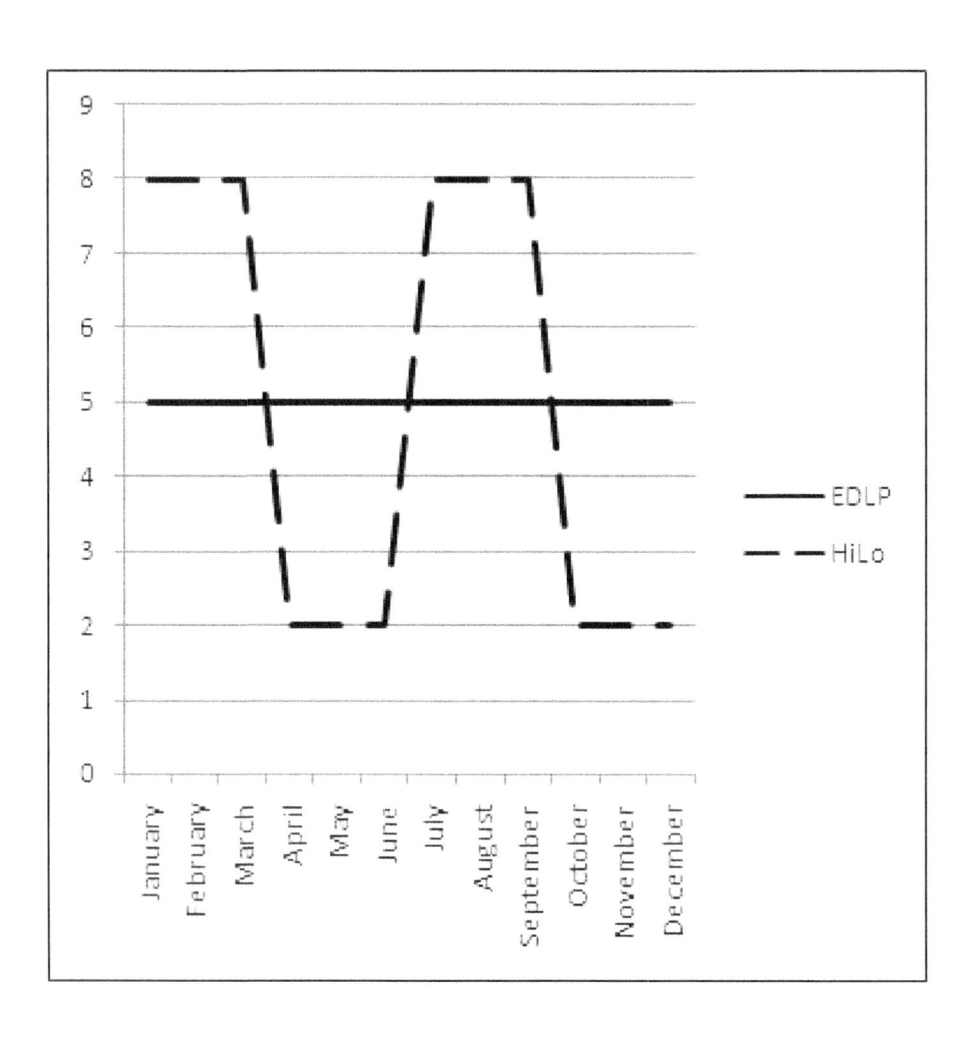

Like EDLP, HiLo also has some restrictions. If customers realise that the retailer will sell the same product at a much lower price at the end of the season or after sometime, then they are most likely to wait for that duration when you sell your products at much lower rate. In such a scenario, sales during high price time are going to reduce rapidly, and ultimately you make profit with a very low margin.

So, deciding the price and the choosing the appropriate strategy is a bit challenging, but if done correctly can optimise your profit. In this chapter, we discussed about pricing strategies. Now it is time to bring customers to your store and promote your business. In the next chapter, we are going to discuss about promotional strategies commonly used by retailers and a **master trick** to attract customers.

Chapter 9: Sale Promotion

Recall our fundamental business model, i.e. AIDAA model. There, the first step was **awareness.** Once you are ready with your retail store, products and other necessary services, you now need to aware people around you about your existence. You now need customers. And for that, we need to sale promotion strategies.

The main goal of sale promotion is to enhance the store image and increase the amount of revenue generated by sale. Next time you visit the market, try to figure out what kind of promotional strategies retailers are using nowadays.

Advertising

This is the most common way of sale promotion. In televisions, radios, newspapers, etc, we come across many retailers who advertise about new deals or discounts they are offering, new products, new services, etc. Sometimes, you may also find emails telling you about new companies, their prices and discounts. These are all examples of advertising. It is very effective if done properly, but at the same time, they are expensive.

There are three types of advertising-

1. **Above The Line (ATL)-** your message is sent to a large number of audiences who might or might not be your target customer group or category. For example- television advertisements and newspaper advertisements. Television and newspapers are, more or less, used by most of the people out there, irrespective of their income status. So if you use these two media to advertise, you are going to reach a large number of audiences. But they are quite expensive compared to other media which focus on a smaller and more specific group of customers.
2. **Below The Line (BTL)-** your message is sent to more targeted and much more identified people. For example, online advertising and SMSs. Online advertising includes emails, short graphic adds on online platforms like YouTube, Facebook, Instagram, etc. It has

many advantages like, you can deliver different messages to different customers, at different point of time. You can modify your message according to your target customer. BTL is also considerably cheaper than ATL. But, it needs time and a lot of experience. For that, generally, retailers hire online marketing experts for this job.
3. **Through The Line (TTL)-** this is the combined use of both ATL and BTL. Some rich retailers use both ATL and BTL for advertising.

After advertising, we have successfully made our target customers aware of our existence. So the first step of AIDAA model is completed. The second step is creating interest in our customers' mind to visit our store and make a purchase. Several techniques are used by retailers for this operation. Some of them are-

1. **Discounts-** people love discounts. Tell them a high price, they are going to deny, you give a discount on that price, they are going to make the purchase right on spot. In order

to promote sales, build a good retail image, and acquire customers initially, retailers often offer very high discounts which may or may not be time limited. Customers, as they find a way to save money, get attracted to your store. But there are also some drawbacks. Putting high discounts reduces your profit margins. Also, putting very high discounts, as discussed earlier, shows that your product is of very cheap quality, which may hamper your retail image and sales.

2. **Coupons-** you might have noticed that some retailers give coupons to customers which can be used for their next purchase from the same store. Coupons are great ways to retain customers as they give good amount of discounts which customers cannot ignore. Sometimes, you might have also noticed one retailer giving coupons of another retailer of another retail type. Let us understand this concept by an example. Suppose there are two retailer, retailer A and retailer B. Retailer A sells ladies garments, while retailer B sells ladies

jewelries. Retailer A offers coupons to his customers which give them a discount of 30% on any purchase from retailer B. At the same time, Retailer B gives his customers coupons of 30% discount on any purchase from retailer A. This strategy helps them get each other's customers, hence the total number of customers in each store increases, so as their sales.

3. **Sweepstakes-** sometimes retailers organise some kind of lottery for their customers. If a customer makes any purchase from the store, he is now requested to pay a little extra and participate in the lottery. The winner gets a very expensive item free of cost. Customers love to get items at a very low rate. But when it is free, they become more excited. So in such cases, most of the customers participate in the lottery. Now, there will be only one winner, but a lot of customers participate. You can use their participation fee to buy that expensive gift. So, you don't actually need to spend much in this strategy.

4. **Frequent shopper's program-** recall our discussion on customer retention rate, and its importance. In order to your customers, retailers often introduces some kind of frequent shopper's program, where retailers offers some special discounts to those customers who make purchases from their retail stores frequently. For example, you might have noticed that some retailers offer huge discounts on their products, exclusively for those customers who had made purchases from their store for certain number times or more. Some other retailer uses the concept of virtual money, where, every time a customer makes any purchase, he is given some virtual money. After having a certain amount of this virtual money, he can redeem it in exchange of a new product. A very good example of this concept is Flipkart's Super Coins.
5. **Referral gifts-** this strategy uses the power of **word of mouth.** When a customer makes a purchase, he is given a referral code and asked to share the code with a certain number of people, say 5. If a new customer

uses that code, he gets a little discount. Once all the 5 new customers shops using the code, the first customer gets a huge cash-back.

These are some commonly used promotional strategies. Next time you visit the market try to find out if there are any other strategies. Also try to form some new strategies of your own.

Master trick!

Even after successfully doing all the necessary advertisements and other sale promotional activities, sometimes it becomes very difficult to actually start driving traffic into the store initially. Think about the first customer. When he comes to the store and finds out that there are no other customers inside, he starts feeling like, there are no customers because the quality of products or services of this store are poor. So he becomes less confident about the store and starts looking for other retailers. This is a problem that many new retailers face.

To cope up with this plan, some retailers use a very simple trick. They hire some people to just visit their store and fill up the store space, so that it looks crowded. By doing this, from outside, it shows that the store is quite famous and doing well with its products and services. So the first real customer, by seeing this, gets the confidence to make a purchase from the store.

But, you need to be very careful during this operation. You should never fill up your store with hired people on the very first day. This may create doubt in actual customer's mind. No store gets so much of customers on the very first day. You need to make it look real. So start with a few numbers of people. Then increase the count gradually. Once you start getting enough real customers, you can now reduce the count gradually. The main focus is to make it look natural.

Many retailers out there are unaware of this trick. But you know this. If required, use the trick.

Note down one important concept before we move on to our next chapter. When you are giving ads for your products, after a certain time, the sales of that product reaches a stagnation point, after which, the sales of that doesn't increase any more even if you keep spending more on ads. You need to identify that stagnation point. Here is a graph which explains this concept-

```
        Sales ▲
              │ ─ ─ ─ ─ ─ ─ ─ ─ ─ ─ ─ ─ ─   Stagnation
              │                    ╱┆
              │                 ╱   ┆
              │              ╱      ┆
              │           ╱         ┆
              │        ╱            ┆
              │     ╱               ┆
              │  ╱                  ┆
              │╱_____┆_____▶
                                        Ad Expenditure
```

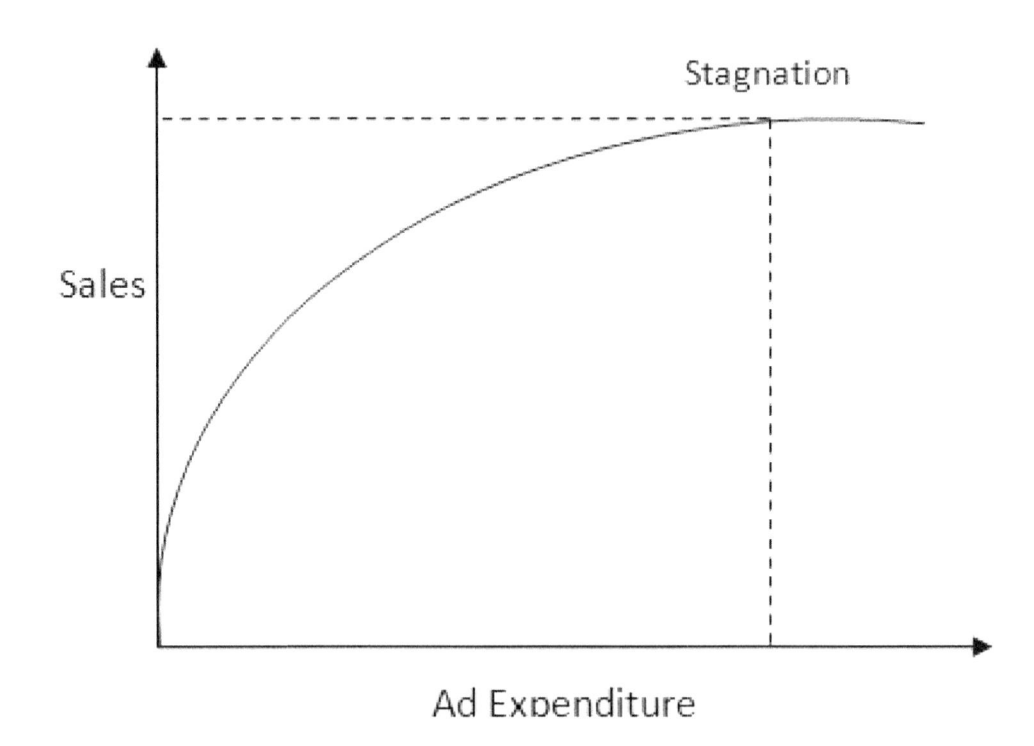

So in this chapter, we learned about how to promote your business and drive traffic in store. Once the customers are in, you now need store staffs to provide them with necessary services. In the next chapter we will discuss on this and understand human resource management.

Chapter 10: HR Management

Now it is time to focus on our employees. When a customer walks in, generally, a sales person or a staff is appointed to guide the customer throughout the purchase process. The customer expects very good behavior and service from that staff. Their performance directly influences your retail image. So it is important to train your staffs or employees very well.

In a retail store, there are generally four kinds of jobs involved-

1. **Store management-** here the assigned person's duty is to manage the entire store operations. His job is to look after the store maintenance, exterior and interior element, overall display, cleanliness etc.
2. **Communications-** these people are assigned to directly communicate with customers, like contacting the customers for post purchase support, describing the product in showroom, etc.

3. **Merchandising-** these people are given the duty to look after merchandises. It is their duty to ensure there is sufficient quantity of products, at the right place, at right time.
4. **Financial and control-** at the end of the day, the only thing that matters is money. These people are assigned to look after financial matters. They are also responsible for sale promotional activities, customer data base management, etc.

In order to have a smooth retail operation, you need to focus on each of these areas very well. While recruiting, you need to understand the potential of your employee and assign him job accordingly.

Now the question is, why do we need a good HR management system in our store? This is because, as discussed earlier, the behavior of your employee towards your customers affects your retail image, so HR management system makes your employee friendlier and makes him behave well. Also, sometimes, due to poor HR management, conflict rises between employees, which may force an employee to leave the job. That is not what we want, because recruiting a new person in his place involves a lot of money and time required to train him.

HR management has two objectives-

1. **Short term objective-** to increase the productivity of employees. Productivity means the number of sales per employee.
2. **Long term objectives-** to make sure your employees do not leave the job as it requires a lot of money to be spent to hire and train new employees.

Four steps involved in HR management system-

1. **Recruiting-** you need to first recruit your employees. You can do this by giving ads about the job on newspapers and ask the candidates to submit their resume to your email and ask them to come at your office for interview.
2. **Training-** now you need to train them so that they can do their duties very well. You need to tell them about your products, about managing accounts, managing

customer's experience, etc. It is often advised to hire an HR management expert for this job.

3. **Compensating-** an employee gives his full effort on his job only when he takes it personally. And your job is to encourage him as much as possible. Compensating is one way of doing it. You need to give them bonus if they show exceptional dedication towards their job. Everybody wants extra money, extra salary, extra income. So if you ensure them for a bonus, they will work very hard to get that extra income. Promotions of employees are important.

4. **Monitoring-** close observation of your employees is very crucial. You need to make sure that your employees are doing their respective jobs according as per your expectation. If not, take necessary actions. Also, it lets you know whether your employees deserve a promotion or not.

One other reason why you need HR management system is to make your retail operation autonomous. Remember the basic characteristic of passive income? You get income without actually working. After you have successfully established your retail organisation, you need to convert it to a source of passive income. Now in case you have a poor HR management system, you need to visit your store frequently to ensure your employees are working accordingly, which doesn't fulfill the basic requirement of passive income.

So in this chapter we basically learned how to handle our employees. In the next chapter we are going to learn about customer relationship and experience management. I advise my readers to kindly make a note of all the topics that we have discussed so far and upcoming topics. Retailing is a vast subject. It needs time to set up, but once done, it gives very high return on investments. Have patience.

Chapter 11: Customer Experience

Customers are the main assets for any retail organisation. Recall the definition of assets. Anything which puts money in your pocket is an asset. Customers are the main source of income for a retail organisation. Thus it is important to invest time and effort on our customers.

Till now we have discussed about acquiring customers and selling them products. Now we are going to talk about customer retention, experience and satisfaction. A customer would like to visit you only when he feels satisfied with his previous experience, likes your retailing system, has a good relationship with your store, and feels more familiar and comfortable. Different customers have different shopping behaviors, hence should be treated differently too. Treating differently doesn't mean that your staffs should behave differently with different customers, but manage their experiences differently.

We can classify our customers on various aspects. For example, according to the type of products they buy, we can classify customers as-

1. **Economic customers-** they look for products which are more affordable. This kind of customer usually waits for great discounts.
2. **Status oriented customers-** these customers are very rich and prefer only high end luxury or costly products. They usually don't care about the price, but experience they get by using the product.
3. **Assortment oriented customers-** these customers are very specific about their required product. They enter the store with a particular product in their mind. They ask for that product, if it is available at the right price, they will buy it immediately, otherwise look for other retailers. You cannot try impulse purchase strategy on them. They are very specific about their needs.
4. **Convenience oriented customers-** these customers do care about experience, but also the price. They need products which

are available at an affordable price and also give a fair experience. They do not necessarily wait for offers or discounts.

Based on the amount of money customers spend, they can be classified as-

1. **Affluent social-** affluent families with young kids. They are rich customers and are ready to pay high prices. They prefer convenience over price and other benefits. They want healthy lifestyle and upscale branded merchandise.
2. **Single nomads-** these are young professionals who have a stable job and good education. They stay away from their homes for the sake of their jobs. They earn a considerably good amount of money and spend accordingly. They are also ready to pay good prices, but lesser than affluent socials.
3. **Jack of all trades-** middle class families. They are trying to make ends meet with a limited budget. They have stable jobs, but education and job profiles are lower than affluent socials and single nomads. They

prefer to chase discounts and offers, and are not interested in premium products.
4. **Fighting toughies-** these are low income customers with unstable jobs, mostly daily wagers who have a tough budget. Purchase cycles involve basic essentials and high frequency. They hunt for discounts and offers.

You can have other classifications too based on the kind of merchandises you are selling. Now, each category of customers spend different amount of money in your store. So the discounts you offer should be different for different categories too in order to generate maximum revenue. For example, if you give only 10% discount for all categories of customers, then, although affluent socials are going to buy the product, even single nomads too, but for jack of all trades and fighting toughies, it becomes less affordable and they start looking for other stores. So, the number of sales is below your optimum level. Now if you put different discounts for different customers, say 10% for affluent socials and single nomads, 25% for jack of all trades and 35% for fighting toughies, then it sounds more affordable for all types of customers, hence they start buying the product and your sales increases, so is the revenue.

But the question is, when a customer visits the store, how to understand his category and how give different offers to different customers?

As discussed in the previous section, different category of customers demand different products, some want high end luxury products, while the others look for more affordable products. Also notice one thing, customers who are looking for expensive products, does not care about the discounts or offers. They just want it. On the other hand, customers who are looking for affordable products are also looking for great discounts or offers. Remember, our goal is to satisfy our customers' needs and give them a better experience. So try to think hard here, if you put little discount on expensive products, you can still sell them as their customers doesn't care about offers. Also, if you put high discounts on cheaper or affordable products, you are able to satisfy the customers who are looking for such products.

So, you don't need to put an extra effort in trying to understand a customer's category. Just put different offers on different products, and when the customer asks for a particular product or gives you his budget, you will automatically get to know about his category.

Building relationships with customers

Recall our AIDAA model. The final step was 'advocacy'. Advocacy is a customer's post purchase behavior, which decides whether he is going to stick to your retail store or switch to some of your competitor. In order to avoid such cases of switching brands or retailers, we need to build a post purchase relationship with the customer.

Many a times, after purchasing a product, customers try to contact you and report a problem or file a complaint against the product, and expect you to solve it as soon as possible. They do so because they want to stick to your store only. If you can take action as soon as possible, you are able to retain your customers, otherwise not. For this, many retailers provide post purchase supports, like a call centre, where a customer can call and report his problem. Necessary actions are then taken.

Sometimes, post purchase offers are also introduced to customers through such post purchase support systems. A staff from the retail organisation calls the customer and gives him offers based on his purchase behavior, based on the kind of products he bought last time, price range he prefers, etc. But, before that, you need to build a good relationship with that customer. Otherwise customers find such sales calls very annoying.

So after purchase, when you call the customer, you need to first ask him about his previous experience, quality of product, whether he likes it or not, any new suggestion, etc. Then tell him about new offers. After you are done, again try to build relationship and make him feel more comfortable with you.

How to get a customer's number? You might have noticed that in the billing counters, the staff asks you for your address and phone number, sometimes even email addresses. This is how you get a customer's contact details. Later on you can even use emails to send him details of some new offers and discount which he may like. We will discuss about this concept more in retail analysis.

Chapter 12: Retail Analysis

Analysis of a business is very important, especially in retailing business. A good analysis of retailing performance gives the retailer a clear knowledge of changes required in investments plans, category of customers and products which need more focus, and other essential areas of improvements. It also gives the retailer advance notice of new business models or model changes.

There are several indicators which retailers use in order to evaluate their retailing performances, like-

1. Net sales
2. Cost of goods sold (COGS)
3. Gross profit
4. Operating expenses
5. Net profit before tax
6. Tax
7. Net profit
8. Average inventory cost
9. Inventory turnover ratio
10. Return on assets

COGS or cost of goods sold is the amount that a retailer needs to invest in order to buy the merchandise he is planning to sell. COGS must be kept as minimum as possible. Lesser the COGS, higher the net profit.

Gross profit is the difference between sales and COGS, simple mathematics.

Gross Profit = Sales – COGS

Gross Margin = (Gross Profit/Sales) X 100%

The goal is to maintain a good amount of gross profit, which can satisfy your operating costs, as well as contribute to your personal income.

A retailing operation involves several costs other than COGS, like store maintenance, electricity and water supply, store design and other investments. These costs are required to be kept as minimum as possible, but make sure that there is no compromise with your customers' satisfaction.

Net profit before tax is the amount of gross profit money that you are left with after paying the bills for all other expenses.

Net profit is the final amount of money that you are left with after paying all of your business taxes. Keep in mind, you need to pay your employees their salaries from this net profit only. So you need to make sure that it is quite a good amount of money, because it has your share too.

Recall the concept of merchandise space. It is nothing but an inventory where merchandises which are not yet sold are kept. The total cost of products which are in your inventory is your **average inventory cost**.

Inventory turnover ratio is the ratio of COGS to average inventory cost

Inventory Turnover Ratio = COGS/Average Inventory Cost

A retail organisation has many assets, like the physical store area, its employees, customers, etc. **return on assets** is the ratio of net profit to the total value of assets.

There are several other indicators as well which can be used for analysis, like- revenue generated from each category of product, each category of customers, sales per employee, revenue generated from one particular discount or offer plan executed earlier, etc.

Revenue generated from each category of products gives a clear picture of which category of customers we need to focus on more. For example, if most of the revenue is generated from jack of all trades, then you need to focus more on this category of customers compared to other categories in order to retain them. Also, the product which generates higher revenues compared to other products must be kept in higher quantities at the store or inventory for sale.

We can gather such information from previous sales records. But how to know about customers' expectations? In one of our earlier sessions we had discussed about the importance of customer satisfaction. For that we need to predict general expectations of a particular category of customers. For that, retailers often take the help of surveys. Recall the concept of post purchase support, building relationships with customers. While calling a customer to get feedback about his previous purchase, the staff can ask him some questions and ask for suggestions. After that, suggestions from different customers from the same category are compared and common suggestions are listed out. The retailer can now work on these suggestions and try to enhance customer experience. Sometimes emails are also used for such surveys.

Till now we have discussed about offline retailing only. In the next chapter we are going to learn about online retailing. It is quite similar to offline retailing, with few changes regarding pricing strategy, operating methods, etc.

Chapter 13: Online Retailing

Online retailing is a mode of retailing where a customer can place an order for a product or products directly from his home. Instead of having physical showroom, in online retailing, retailers have online platforms where products are displayed virtually. A very good example is Amazon. Retailers can have their own online store or can also sale on platforms like Amazon.

You might have often noticed that a product which is available at a physical store is available at much lesser price on online stores. Ever wondered why is this so? There are several reasons behind this-

i. Since there is no physical store, the retailer needs not to pay for the physical land itself.
ii. This there is no physical store, no property tax needs to be paid.
iii. Store maintenance cost is zero.
iv. No physical store means lesser number of employees required.

v. The retailer only needs to pay for building the online platform and its maintenance, which is much cheaper than in the case of physical store.

For these reasons, expenses of retailer reduce a lot. Thus, he is able to sell his products at lesser price on online store as compared to offline physical stores.

There are several advantages as well as disadvantages of online retailing.

Advantages-

i. As discussed earlier, online retailing involves much lesser amount of investments as compared to offline retailing.
ii. Online platforms can be used to collect a customer's contacts even if he doesn't make any purchase. For example, some online stores, once you visit their website, they immediately ask you to make an account in their website using either your phone number or email. Once you enter your details, the retailer can use them to

send you information about new deals, offers or discounts.
iii. Since online prices are much lesser than offline stores, greater numbers of customers are expected in online platforms. As a result, higher numbers of sales are also expected.
iv. Due to limited space in offline stores, limited products are put on display. But in online stores, due to unlimited space, a lot of varieties and assortments of products can be displayed.
v. With the use of 'filter' feature, a customer can easily find the product of his convenience. This contributes to customer experience and satisfaction.

Disadvantages-

i. There are some products which customers prefer to touch and feel before buying, such as textiles or garments. They want to make sure that the quality of the product is very fine. In online retailing, this is not possible.
ii. Online websites are vulnerable to hackers and viruses. They can misuse it. So a retailer

needs to pay extra for keeping the system updated and risk free.
iii. Online stores often offer the facility of returning the product to the retailer with zero service cost within certain days if the customer is not satisfied with the product. In such scenarios the retailer faces considerable amount of loss.
iv. Aged customers often find it difficult to use online media as they are not so much used to modern technologies. They still prefer physical stores.

Depending upon the kind of merchandise a retailer plans to sell, the choice of either having a physical store or an online platform is made. Before starting your business, try to understand what your competitors are doing. Learn from them, and figure out which method you should go for.

There are several formats of online retailing. When a customer puts an order, you can directly deliver the product from the manufacturer or supplier to the customer. Also, just like physical stores, you can have your own merchandise space, where you first buy the products and store them in your inventory. Later on when a customer puts an order, you can deliver the product from your inventory. Sometimes, retailers use both of these methods in order to maximize their profit.

Now a days, some retailers use both offline and online platforms and try to ustilise advantages of both the channels. Such a form of retailing is called **Omni channel retailing.** In India, a very good example of such companies is Lenskart. It has both physical stores and an online store. In omni channel retailing, the online platform is used as a catalogue by the customers to know which products you are selling. Then, if your products fall into their list of requirements, they can either order the product online, or if they want to see or physically touch the product, they can visit the physical store. Such a way of business is a bit complicated, but often very profitable.

Before you start online business, build your website by an expert only. Also, there are some legal activities which are to be done. I am not an expert in that, so I would suggest you to consult with a person who is experienced regarding legal works.

With this, we are ending our discussion on retailing business. I hope my readers have gone through the entire book thoroughly and understood it very well.

Chapter 14: Case Study

Now, to wrap up all the concepts discussed previously and how to execute them, let us understand via a real life case study.

We are going to take the case of **DMart**. Founded by Radhakishan Damani in the year 2002, Dmart is India's most successful chain of hypermarkets. As of 21 November 2019, the market capitalization of DMart is close to ₹114,000 crore, making it the 33rd largest company listed on the Bombay Stock Exchange. By the year 2010, it had 25 stores, which grew to over 200 stores by 2021. And the best part, none of them closed.

Along with DMart, we will also discuss about **Future Retail**, which is another leading retailer that operates multiple retail formats in both value and lifestyle segment of Indian consumer market, but struggling financially lately. On 17th March 2021, share price of Dmart was around Rs 3000, whereas the share price of Future Retail is Rs 64.55. We will compare them, go through various parameters and try to understand why Dmart is so successful, while Future Retail is still struggling.

DMart's 7 Strategies

1. Strong Fundamentals
2. Slotting Fee
3. Control on Operating Expenses
4. Pricing Strategy
5. Local Products
6. Correct Store Location
7. Organic Expansion

Strong fundamentals

Recall what we had discussed at the first few chapters about fundamentals of retailing. For a successful retail business its fundamentals should be strong. This includes your targeted audience or market segment, your product and pricing based on the targeted market segment. Dmart has always kept its fundamentals strong and unchanged. It targets the middle class people, who look for offers and heavy discounts and relatively good quality.

Based on its targeted market, DMart takes further action. DMart offers heavy discounts on products throughout the year (EDLP), and yet makes heavy profits. But the question is HOW? How is DMart able to give so high discounts and yet make huge profits? That brings us to its 2nd strategy.

Slotting Fee

One reason why manufacturers love selling their products to DMart because DMart is able to pay the purchase price to the manufacturers within 30 days, whereas in case of Big Bazaar (a subsidiary of Future Retail) takes 90 days. This means a faster cash flow for the manufacturers.

That is why manufacturers approach DMart for selling their products DMart takes the advantage of this situation. DMart asks the manufacturer to pay DMart a **slotting fee** to keep their products in the middle shelves in the store, which as you know gets more attention from customer and thus tends to sell more and faster. Manufacturers pay the slotting fee. Because of this cash DMart is able to further reduce the selling price, which is of course more appealing to its customers.

So, this strategy is a *win-win* situation for both the manufacturer and DMart.

Control on Operating Expenses

What is the first way to increase the profit that comes in your mind? To reduce the expenses, right? That is what DMart also does. If you visit any DMart store, you will see that the overall design or ambience of the store is very simple. There's no air conditioner, no fancy lighting, no fancy sitting area, nothing of that sort, because its customers are there for heavy discounts and not for hanging out. This makes the store much easier to maintain, keeping the operating expenses low, hence increasing the profit. This again helps DMart to further reduce the price of products.

Pricing Strategy

DMart sells products which are of everyday use. Hence, customers will be coming quite frequently. At the same time these customers expect good discounts everyday they visit the store. What do you think, what will be the ideal pricing strategy for DMart? Is is EDLP or HiLo?

Yes, you are right, it should be EDLP. And DMart executes the EDLP strategy only. If you compare this Future Retail, it follows HiLo strategy, yet targets customers similar to that of DMart. This is a reason why Future Retails performances are so poor.

Local Products

One fundamental goal of DMart is to sell the products as soon as possible. It observed that customers tend to buy products which are famous in that locality. That is why DMart keeps popular local products in its store.

Correct Store Location

One feature of the targeted customers of DMart is that they although they have less income but have sufficient time and are ready to travel far in order to save a few bucks. This is quite common in middle class families, isn't it? DMart takes the advantage of this feature.

Instead of buying stores in the heart of the city or in shopping malls, DMart sets up its stores a little distance away from the city, where land plots are relatively cheaper. It knows that, even though the store is away from the city's heart, its customers will take that extra pain to visit the store for those heavy discounts.

Many retailers nowadays have moved toward online retailing, but not DMart. It still follows the traditional brick and mortar format, because its customers still believes in and enjoys purchasing in bulk from physical stores.

Organic Expansion

One exciting feature of DMart is that it doesn't take any loan for setting up new stores. At the beginning the profits generated from one store was used to set up another store. Later on, profits from these two stores were used to open two more store, and so on. That is why all the stores of DMart are actually owned by DMart itself.

This is the reason why DMart's profits are so high compared to Future retail, though there is not much of a difference between the revenues of these two.

...The End...

Printed in Great Britain
by Amazon